WILMA
RUDOLPH

WILMA RUDOLPH

TOM BIRACREE

CHELSEA HOUSE PUBLISHERS

PHILADELPHIA

EDITOR-IN-CHIEF: Nancy Toff
EXECUTIVE EDITOR: Remmel T. Nunn
MANAGING EDITOR: Karyn Gullen Browne
COPY CHIEF: Juliann Barbato
PICTURE EDITOR: Adrian G. Allen
ART DIRECTOR: Giannella Garrett
MANUFACTURING MANAGER: Gerald Levine

Staff for WILMA RUDOLPH:

SENIOR EDITOR: Constance Jones
ASSISTANT EDITOR: Maria Behan
EDITORIAL ASSISTANT: Theodore Keyes
COPYEDITORS: Terrance Dolan, Ellen Scordato
PICTURE RESEARCHER: Diane Wallis
DESIGNER: Design Oasis
PRODUCTION COORDINATOR: Joseph Romano
COVER ILLUSTRATION: Liane Fried

CREATIVE DIRECTOR: Harold Steinberg

15 14

Library of Congress Cataloging in Publication Data

Biracree, Tom, 1947–
  Wilma Rudolph.

  (American women of achievement)
  Bibliography: p.
  Includes index.
  Summary: A biography of the woman who overcame crippling
polio as a child to become the first woman to win three gold
medals in track in a single Olympics.
    1. Rudolph, Wilma, 1940–   —Juvenile literature. 2. Athletes—
United States—Biography—Juvenile literature.
[1. Rudolph, Wilma, 1940–   . 2. Track and field athletes.
3. Afro-Americans—Biography]
I. Title.   II. Series.
GV697.R8B57   1987   796.4'2'0924 [B] [92]   87-15138

ISBN 1-55546-675-3
      0-7910-0217-9 (pbk.)

CONTENTS

WOMEN of ACHIEVEMENT

Abigail Adams
WOMEN'S RIGHTS ADVOCATE

Jane Addams
SOCIAL WORKER

Madeleine Albright
STATESWOMAN

Louisa May Alcott
AUTHOR

Marian Anderson
SINGER

Susan B. Anthony
SUFFRAGETTE

Ethel Barrymore
ACTRESS

Clara Barton
AMERICAN RED CROSS FOUNDER

Elizabeth Blackwell
PHYSICIAN

Margaret Bourke-White
PHOTOGRAPHER

Pearl Buck
AUTHOR

Rachel Carson
BIOLOGIST AND AUTHOR

Mary Cassatt
ARTIST

Hillary Rodham Clinton
FIRST LADY/ATTORNEY

Agnes de Mille
CHOREOGRAPHER

Diana, Princess of Wales
HUMANITARIAN

Emily Dickinson
POET

Elizabeth Dole
POLITICIAN

Isadora Duncan
DANCER

Amelia Earhart
AVIATOR

Jodie Foster
ACTRESS/DIRECTOR

Betty Friedan
FEMINIST

Althea Gibson
TENNIS CHAMPION

Ruth Bader Ginsburg
SUPREME COURT JUSTICE

Helen Hayes
ACTRESS

Katharine Hepburn
ACTRESS

Anne Hutchinson
RELIGIOUS LEADER

Mahalia Jackson
GOSPEL SINGER

Helen Keller
HUMANITARIAN

Jeane Kirkpatrick
DIPLOMAT

Barbara McClintock
BIOLOGIST

Margaret Mead
ANTHROPOLOGIST

Edna St. Vincent Millay
POET

Julia Morgan
ARCHITECT

Grandma Moses
PAINTER

Lucretia Mott
SUFFRAGETTE

Sandra Day O'Connor
SUPREME COURT JUSTICE

Rosie O'Donnell
ENTERTAINER/COMEDIAN

Georgia O'Keeffe
PAINTER

Eleanor Roosevelt
DIPLOMAT AND HUMANITARIAN

Wilma Rudolph
CHAMPION ATHLETE

Elizabeth Cady Stanton
SUFFRAGETTE

Gloria Steinem
FEMINIST

Harriet Beecher Stowe
AUTHOR AND ABOLITIONIST

Barbra Streisand
ENTERTAINER

Elizabeth Taylor
ACTRESS/ACTIVIST

**Abigail Van Buren/
Ann Landers**
COLUMNISTS

Barbara Walters
JOURNALIST

Edith Wharton
AUTHOR

Phyllis Wheatley
POET

Babe Didrikson Zaharias
CHAMPION ATHLETE

"Remember the Ladies"

MATINA S. HORNER

Remember the Ladies." That is what Abigail Adams wrote to her husband John, then a delegate to the Continental Congress, as the Founding Fathers met in Philadelphia to form a new nation in March of 1776. "Be more generous and favorable to them than your ancestors. Do not put such unlimited power in the hands of the Husbands. If particular care and attention is not paid to the Ladies," Abigail Adams warned, "we are determined to foment a Rebellion, and will not hold ourselves bound by any Laws in which we have no voice, or Representation."

The words of Abigail Adams, one of the earliest American advocates of women's rights, were prophetic. Because when we have not "remembered the ladies," they have, by their words and deeds, reminded us so forcefully of the omission that we cannot fail to remember them. For the history of American women is as interesting and varied as the history of our nation as a whole. American women have played an integral part in founding, settling, and building our country. Some we remember as remarkable women who—against great odds—achieved distinction in the public arena: Anne Hutchinson, who in the 17th century became a charismatic religious leader; Phillis Wheatley, an 18th-century black slave who became a poet; Susan B. Anthony, whose name is synonymous with the 19th-century women's rights movement, and who led the struggle to enfranchise women; and, in our own century, Amelia Earhart, the first woman to cross the Atlantic Ocean by air.

These extraordinary women certainly merit our admiration, but other women, "common women," many of them all but forgotten, should also be recognized for their contributions to American thought and culture. Women have been community builders; they have founded schools and formed voluntary associations to help those in need; they have assumed the major responsibility for rearing children, passing on from one generation to the next the values that keep a culture alive. These and innumerable other contributions, once ignored, are now being recognized by scholars, students, and the public. It is exciting and gratifying to realize that a part of our history that was hardly acknowledged a few generations ago is now being studied and brought to light.

In recent decades, the field of women's history has grown from obscurity to a politically controversial splinter movement to academic respectability, in many cases mainstreamed into such traditional disciplines as history, economics, and psychology. Scholars of women, both female and male, have organized research centers at such prestigious institutions as Wellesley College, Stanford University, and the University of California. Other notable centers for women's studies are the Center for the American Woman and Politics at the Eagleton Institute of Politics at Rutgers University, the Henry A. Murray Research Center for the Study of Lives, at Radcliffe College, and the Women's Research and Education Institute, the research arm of the Congressional Caucus on Women's Issues. Other scholars and public figures have established archives and libraries, such as the Schlesinger Library on the History of Women in America, at Radcliffe College, and the Sophia Smith Collection, at Smith College, to collect and preserve the written and tangible legacies of women.

From the initial donation of the Women's Rights Collection in 1943, the Schlesinger Library grew to encompass vast collections documenting the manifold accomplishments of American women. Simultaneously, the women's movement in general and the academic discipline of women's studies in particular also began with a narrow definition and gradually expanded their mandate. Early causes such as woman suffrage and social reform, abolition and organized labor were joined by newer concerns such as the history of women in business and the professions and in politics and government; the study of the family; and social issues such as health policy and education.

Women, as historian Arthur M. Schlesinger, jr., once pointed out, "have constituted the most spectacular casualty of traditional history. They have made up at least half the human race, but you could never tell that by looking at the books historians write." The new breed of historians is remedying that omission. They have written books about immigrant women and about work-ing-class women who struggled for survival in cities and about black women who met the challenges of life in rural areas. They are telling the stories of women who, despite the barriers of tradition and economics, became lawyers and doctors and public figures.

The women's studies movement has also led scholars to question tradi-tional interpretations of their respective disciplines. For example, the study of war has traditionally been an exercise in military and political analysis, an examination of strategies planned and executed by men. But scholars of women's history have pointed out that wars have also been periods of tre-mendous change and even opportunity for women, because the very absence of men on the home front enabled them to expand their educational, eco-nomic, and professional activities and to assume leadership in their homes.

The early scholars of women's history showed a unique brand of courage in choosing to investigate new subjects and take new approaches to old ones. Often, like their subjects, they endured criticism and even ostracism by their academic colleagues. But their efforts have unquestionably been worthwhile, because with the publication of each new study and book another piece of the historical patchwork is sewn into place, revealing an increasingly com-prehensive picture of the role of women in our rich and varied history.

Such books on groups of women are essential, but books that focus on the lives of individuals are equally indispensable. Biographies can be inspirational, offering their readers the example of people with vision who have looked outside themselves for their goals and have often struggled against great obstacles to achieve them. Marian Anderson, for instance, had to overcome racial bigotry in order to perfect her art and perform as a concert singer. Isadora Duncan defied the rules of classical dance to find true artistic free-dom. Jane Addams had to break down society's notions of the proper role for women in order to create new social institutions, notably the settlement house. All of these women had to come to terms both with themselves and with the world in which they lived. Only then could they move ahead as pioneers in their chosen callings.

Biography can inspire not only by adulation but also by realism. It helps us to see not only the qualities in others that we hope to emulate, but also, perhaps, the weaknesses that made them "human." By helping us identify with the subject on a more personal level they help us to feel that we, too, can achieve such goals. We read about Eleanor Roosevelt, for instance, who occupied a unique and seemingly enviable position as the wife of the pres-ident. Yet we can sympathize with her inner dilemma: an inherently shy woman, she had to force herself to live a most public life in order to use her position to benefit others. We may not be able to imagine ourselves having the immense poetic talent of Emily Dickinson, but from her story we can understand the challenges faced by a creative woman who was expected to fulfill many family responsibilities. And though few of us will ever reach the level of athletic accomplishment displayed by Wilma Rudolph or Babe Zaharias, we can still appreciate their spirit, their overwhelming will to excel.

A biography is a multifaceted lens. It is first of all a magnification, the intimate examination of one particular life. But at the same time, it is a wide-angle lens, informing us about the world in which the subject lived. We come away from reading about one life knowing more about the social, political, and economic fabric of the time. It is for this reason, perhaps, that the great New England essayist Ralph Waldo Emerson wrote, in 1841, "There is properly no history: only biography." And it is also why biography, and particularly women's biography, will continue to fascinate writers and readers alike.

WILMA RUDOLPH

Wilma Rudolph stretches her famed long legs as she prepares for competition. The star of the U.S. women's track team, she captured three gold medals at the 1960 Olympic Games.

ONE

The Fastest Woman in the World

On the morning of September 7, 1960, Rome was blistering hot. Yet as the temperature climbed toward 100 degrees, 80,000 spectators jammed the *Stadio Olympico*, site of the 1960 Summer Olympic Games. It was the final day of track-and-field competition, and they were hoping to see history made.

Below the stadium, athletes were crowded in the tunnels that led to the field. Some talked quietly with teammates and coaches. Others paced or repeated their warm-ups to shed their nervous energy. The longer they waited in the stifling heat, the more intense their anxiety grew.

But one athlete seemed oblivious to all the tension and confusion. A tall black woman wearing the red, white, and blue uniform of the U.S. team sat serenely by herself, as unaffected by the commotion as if she were in a cocoon. Her composure was especially remarkable because she was the center of attention that day. In little more than a week, shy, 20-year-old Wilma Rudolph had risen from obscurity to become the most popular of the 6,000 athletes from 84 countries competing in the Olympic Games.

The roots of this international competition stretched back nearly 3,000 years. The ancient Greeks gathered for the first recorded Olympic festival in 776 B.C. The athletic contests were such a mainstay of their culture that the Greeks based their calendar on *Olympiads*—the four-year span between games. The ancient Olympics continued for more than 1,000 years until the Christian emperor Theodosius abolished the event because of its

A young Greek woman, immortalized in stone, runs a footrace. When the Greeks began the Olympic competition in 776 B.C., females were forbidden to participate or act as spectators.

Eager crowds enter the stadium for the first modern Olympics, held in Athens, Greece, in 1896. The arena was a restored structure where many of the ancient Olympics had taken place.

origins in the "pagan" Greek religion.

The first modern Olympics were held in Athens, Greece, in 1896. They were organized by Baron Pierre de Coubertin, a French educator who hoped the competition would foster international understanding. Only eight nations entered that first year. But soon the modern Olympic Games, held every four years just like their ancient counterparts, became the world's most prestigious athletic spectacle, attracting thousands of competitors from dozens of nations.

Track, or the running of foot races, was the oldest and most popular of Olympic sports. The very first event in the ancient Olympics was a 200-yard race to determine the swiftest man in Greece. In the modern Olympics, two track events—the 100-meter dash and the 200-meter dash—decide which su-

Rudolph breaks the tape to finish first in the 100-meter semifinal at the 1960 Olympics in Rome. Her smooth, effortless running style was especially remarkable because she had been crippled by polio in earlier years.

perb athletes will hold the coveted titles of "fastest man in the world" and "fastest woman in the world."

A gold medal is the highest honor an Olympic athlete can receive, and Rudolph had already captured two of them. She had run the 100-meter dash in an impressive 11 seconds flat. She also had won the 200-meter dash in 23.2 seconds, a new Olympic record. After these twin triumphs, she was being hailed throughout the world as "the fastest woman in history."

And today she would compete as a member of the 4-woman U.S. team in the 400-meter relay. A U.S. victory would make her the first American woman runner ever to win three gold medals at a single Olympics.

Rudolph had a special, personal reason to hope for a victory—to pay tribute to Jesse Owens, the celebrated black athlete who had been her inspiration. The star of the 1936 Winter Olympic Games, held in Berlin, Germany, Owens had competed under conditions that could not have been more hostile. At that time, Germany was controlled by dictator Adolf Hitler. One of the key beliefs of Hitler's Nazi party was that his nation's people, predominantly blond, blue-eyed Christians, were biologically superior to the members of other racial and ethnic groups, especially Jews and blacks.

Hitler had boasted that the Olympics would prove the "racial superiority" of the Germans, and his arrogance swelled when German athletes won the first events in the games. But then the American track-and-field team, led by Jesse Owens, began to gain ground. Competing before screaming, taunting crowds, Owens set a world record in the broad jump. Then he buried his German competitors successively in the 100-meter dash, the 200-meter dash, and the 400-meter relay. At the same time, 10 of the other 11 black athletes on the American team won at least 1 first-, second-, or third-place medal. Furious, Adolf Hitler refused to shake the triumphant Owens's hand, but the point had been made: Black athletes, whom Hitler considered "subhuman," had triumphed over Germany's supposedly "superior" contenders.

In the years following the 1936 Olympics, Owens's example inspired blacks to overcome the obstacles and prejudices that held them back not only in sports but in nearly every area of life. So on that sweltering September day in Rome, 20-year-old Wilma Rudolph was determined to honor Jesse Owens by bringing home gold medals in the same 3 racing events he had won 24 years earlier.

Finally, it was time for the competitors in the women's 400-meter relay to enter the stadium. The eight four-woman teams marched out of the dark tunnel into the sun-drenched amphitheater. As Rudolph appeared, she was greeted with a chant that had become a familiar refrain at the Rome Olympics: "Vil-ma! Vil-ma! Vil-ma!" From her very first race, Rudolph's calm dedication and graceful speed had made her a crowd favorite, and the spectators let her know it every time she stepped out onto the field.

The crowd of 80,000 spectators in the Stadio Olympico was more than double the population of Wilma Rudolph's hometown of Clarksville, Tennessee. She knew that, in addition,

Adolf Hitler's Nazi government stages an elaborate ceremony on the opening day of the 1936 Olympics. Hitler bragged that German victories in the games would bear out his theories of Aryan racial superiority, but the stellar performances of American black athletes dashed this hope.

Jesse Owens practices the broad jump aboard an ocean liner carrying U.S. athletes to the 1936 Olympics in Berlin. His dignity and determination amid the racist atmosphere surrounding that contest would inspire black athletes around the world, including Wilma Rudolph.

more than 100 million people were watching her on television as she went through her final warm-up exercises. Yet, like Jesse Owens before her, Rudolph had a reserve of quiet strength that enabled her to maintain a firm resolve, even under the most intense pressures.

The odds against a U.S. victory in the pivotal 400-meter relay were daunting—the favored teams were those from the Soviet Union, Great Britain, and, ironically, West Germany. The West German team was led by Jutta Heine, a willowy six-foot-tall blond whom Rudolph considered the most dangerous runner in the field. If Heine got an edge, her long, loping stride would make her very difficult for Rudolph to catch.

Her opponents were not the only runners affecting Rudolph's chances of winning her third gold medal. The performance of her teammates was vitally important. A relay race is a symphony of intricate movements, each of which must fall into place like notes in a musical score. Just as one wrong note can ruin a piece of music, any one of an infinite number of small mishaps can turn a winning relay team into losers.

The relay begins with the first of the four competitors on each team poised on the starting blocks. A bad start in a race decided by tenths of a second can ruin a team's chances. More than one false start—moving before the starter's

Wilma Rudolph and U.S. basketball star Walt Bellamy stroll through Rome's Olympic Village during a break in the competition.

The top runners in the 100-meter dash engage in a 3-way handshake. Second- and third-place finishers Dorothy Hyman (left) and Giuseppina Leone flank the race's winner, Wilma Rudolph.

pistol officially begins the race—can result in disqualification.

The race itself is one complete lap around a 400-meter track, with each team member running a 100-meter leg. Sprinting at over 20 miles per hour, each runner must stay in her curving, 3-foot-wide lane without stumbling. Then, as she completes her leg, she must pass a baton, a 12-inch cylinder, to a teammate who must seize it while accelerating to full speed for the next leg of the race.

The coordination required between teammates must be so precise that relay runners routinely endure endless practice sessions. Rudolph and her three teammates—Martha Hudson, Barbara Jones, and Lucinda Williams— had one major advantage: They were already finely attuned partners. They had made up the winning 400-meter

Wilma Rudolph breaks into a triumphant smile after winning the 200-meter dash. Third-place runner Dorothy Hyman stands on her left; second-place finisher Jutta Heine is on her right.

relay team at Tennessee State University. All the U.S. team had to do today was repeat what they had already executed hundreds of times before.

But the four women had never performed under the pressure of the Olympic Games—pressure that was compounded by the excitement of the

crowd cheering the other events conducted simultaneously in the stadium's infield. Then, too, in the preliminary heats (qualifying races) of the men's and women's relays, seven highly trained teams had already been disqualified. One lapse in concentration by Rudolph and her partners could make their team the eighth.

And a week before this climactic race, Rudolph had twisted her ankle. Somehow, she had still managed to best her opponents in the 100-meter dash the next day, and the 200-meter contest the day after. But those races had been run on straight tracks, whereas the relay was run on a challenging, curved course that put a punishing strain on a runner's ankles. Occasional twinges of pain reminded Rudolph that one slightly misplaced step could send her crashing to the cinders.

The starter called the runners to the starting blocks. Rudolph took her place near the 300-meter mark of the 400-meter track. She always ran "anchor" (the final leg of the race), partly because she was the team's fastest run-

After inching past Soviet runner Irina Press (left), Rudolph captures the 400-meter relay and her third gold medal. Although she had fumbled the baton during the handoff, Rudolph pulled out all the stops to catch up and win the race for the United States.

ner and partly because her one shortcoming as a racer was her inability to make a perfect start from the blocks. That weakness had bothered her a great deal until she learned that Jesse Owens had also been a poor starter who relied on later bursts of speed for his triumphs.

Rudolph knelt to check her track shoes one more time. Suddenly, the crowd grew silent, and without looking she knew the race was about to begin. The crack of the starter's pistol was followed instantaneously by the roar of the spectators.

The runners, sprinting like thoroughbreds, completed the first 100 meters in a little more than 11 seconds without a clear leader emerging. But by the time the second American runner, Barbara Jones, passed the baton to Lucinda Williams, it was clear that the experts had been wrong: The U.S. team had a good chance of capturing the race.

As Williams hurtled toward her, Wilma Rudolph studied the competition. The West German anchor, Jutta Heine, had easily outstripped her opponents in a preliminary race, and Rudolph knew that Heine would be gunning for a victory today. She also knew that Irina Press, a powerfully built sprinter from the Soviet Union, would also be a formidable competitor. When Rudolph saw that Lucinda Williams had come abreast of the West

German and Russian racers, she felt a small surge of relief. It looked as if she would not have to chase Heine and Press.

But disaster struck during the hand-off, when Rudolph fumbled and nearly dropped the baton. She regained control scarcely a foot before reaching the point where the American team would have been disqualified. Rudolph was still in the race, but the U.S. team had fallen behind.

For Rudolph, the final 90 meters of the race seemed to be run in slow motion. Every fiber of strength she had built up in seven years of intensive training was put to the test. She fixed her gaze fiercely on the backs of the other runners as she closed the gap inch by inch.

Coming into the final stretch, she was still two meters behind Irina Press, who had taken the lead. But Rudolph dug down for extra reserves of power. Pushing for the tape that stretched across the finish line, she made a final, desperate lunge. The Soviet runner dropped from sight as Rudolph burst through the tape and collapsed to the ground.

An instant later she was joined by her teammates. They hugged her, sobbing, as they waited for the judges to examine photographs of the finish. The agitated crowd hushed as the announcement blared over the loudspeaker—the U.S. team had won! They

"The Tennessee Tornado," Wilma Rudolph, proudly displays her three gold medals. Her successes in 1960 made her the first American woman to win three track events in a single Olympics.

had triumphed by inches, to set a new record time of 44.5 seconds.

Wilma Rudolph, a shy black woman from a small town in Tennessee, had become the most celebrated female athlete in the world. In carrying out her tribute to Jesse Owens, she had become the first American woman runner to win three gold medals at an Olympic meet. And in reaching her dream, she instilled hope in millions of aspiring female athletes, black and white, across the United States. But her triumphs in the 1960 Olympic Games were all the more amazing because she had surmounted almost impossible barriers to achieve them—obstacles that had even threatened her life.

Crippled by polio at the age of four, Wilma Rudolph was unable to walk without a leg brace for the next several years. A testament to her remarkable dedication, this photo shows her at age 20, just after she became "the fastest woman alive."

TWO

Wilma's Greatest Battles

Wilma Rudolph's first great accomplishment was simply living to see her first birthday. On June 23, 1940, she became the 20th of the 22 children born to Blanche and Ed Rudolph. Her entrance into the world was nearly two months early, a result of a fall suffered by her mother. At birth, she weighed only four and a half pounds, and for a while, it did not look as if she would survive.

Modern science has since given doctors better tools to care for new babies, but in 1940 many infants died at birth. Premature babies such as Wilma faced even higher risks; given the finest medical care available, only half of the babies born in 1940 weighing less than five pounds survived. And the finest medical care was available to very few in those days. The United States was just emerging from the Great Depression, a decade of widespread poverty, when more than 12 million Americans could not find steady work.

Wilma's parents were more fortunate than some, because they did have jobs. Her father eked out a meager living as a railroad porter and handyman. Her mother took in laundry and sewing and worked occasionally as a maid for wealthy white families. In her autobiography, *Wilma*, Rudolph wrote, "My parents' combined income in a single year never amounted to more than $2,500. There was welfare back then, too, but we were never on it because my mother and my father were too proud to be taking handouts from anybody."

The family did without many things that most people consider necessities today. Their little house had no bathroom, only an outhouse a few steps

A young boy sits outside temporary living quarters built after his family lost its home in the Great Depression. The Rudolphs were poor, but they managed to scrape by during this period of widespread financial hardship.

Southern men drink from segregated drinking fountains. Rudolph later wrote that, during her youth, "None of us at the time did very much thinking about the black experience in America, the very thing we were going to have to face when we grew up."

from their back door. New store-bought clothes were rare; Wilma and her brothers and sisters usually wore clothes their mother made for them from patterned flour sacks. Rudolph remembered, "We didn't have too much money back then, but we had everything else, especially love."

Still, life was far from easy for the Rudolph family and especially difficult because they were black. American blacks, particularly in the South, were denied many basic civil rights. Clarksville, Tennessee, a town of approximately 40,000 people, was 75 percent white. The town had several restaurants, but blacks could eat in only one. Public drinking fountains were installed in pairs, offering the same water from the same pipes—but only one could be used by blacks, and if it happened to be out of order, they

could not drink at all. As in other southern towns, Clarksville blacks attended a separate school that was forced to operate on an inadequate budget. Educational opportunities for blacks were so limited that in the year Rudolph was born, only 7 percent of all black adults had graduated from high school. In 1940, Martin Luther King, Jr. (who would later become a champion of racial equality), was still in grammar school, and it would be 14 years before the Supreme Court decided in *Brown v. Board of Education* that racially segregated facilities denied children their constitutional rights.

Because of segregation, Wilma was four or five when she first realized that "there were a lot of white people in this world, and that they belonged to a world that was nothing at all like the world we black people lived in." When she was about six, Rudolph recalls, "I said to myself, 'There's something not right about all this. White folks got all the luxury, and we black folks got the dirty work.' I made up my mind right then and there. 'Wilma,' I said to myself, 'you ain't never gonna be serving

Men gather on the porch of a "Colored Only" bar. Rudolph later recalled that Clarksville's poor blacks would gather in the Hole in the Wall tavern to "drink and listen to the blues music and forget all about their terrible existences."

coffee to no white folks in bed on Saturday mornings.' "

Discrimination also meant poor medical care for blacks—and in her early years, Wilma needed quite a bit of medical attention. As she wrote in her autobiography, "Being a premature baby may explain why I was sick all of the time when I was growing up. I was so skinny, and I never had the strength the other kids had. I would get a common cold, and it would last for weeks, and then it would develop into something else. I was the most sickly child in all of Clarksville." Unfortunately, the town had only 1 black doctor, and the nearest hospital for blacks was 50 miles away in Nashville, the state capital.

Because of the expense and difficulty of obtaining professional medical care, Wilma's mother usually treated her ailing child at home. Rudolph remembered that during her youth, "My mother used to have all of these home remedies she would make herself, and I lived on them. She was very big on hot toddys. That was a concoction of liquor, corn, sugar and a few things that she would cook on the stove.... Another thing my mother was big on was making me sweat. She would pile blanket on top of blanket and make me get under them and sweat." As Rudolph wryly noted in her autobiography, "You're not gonna be no perfect physical specimen living on hot toddys and sweating all the time."

Fortified only by Mrs. Rudolph's folk remedies and her own strong will to survive, Wilma battled against the common childhood diseases that were deadly then, before there were vaccines and drugs to fight them. In the first three years of life, she suffered from measles, mumps, and chicken pox. At age four, she nearly died during a long struggle, first with double pneumonia, then with scarlet fever. Wilma finally recovered, but there was something wrong with her left leg: It was crooked and her foot turned inward. When Mrs. Rudolph took Wilma to see a doctor, she was told that her daughter must have contracted polio during this last long bout with sickness.

Polio is a virus that attacks the central nervous system, causing its victims to lose control over some or all of their muscles. In some cases, it affects the muscles that control breathing, a condition that once caused thousands of deaths every year. Wilma escaped this consequence of the disease, but like many other polio victims, she was left partially paralyzed. The doctors said that her chances of recovering the use of her leg were slim. But as Rudolph told a journalist years later, her mother was determined that Wilma would defy the odds, "The doctors told me I would never walk, but my mother told me I would, so I believed in my mother."

Beginning in 1946, Mrs. Rudolph and Wilma traveled twice a week without

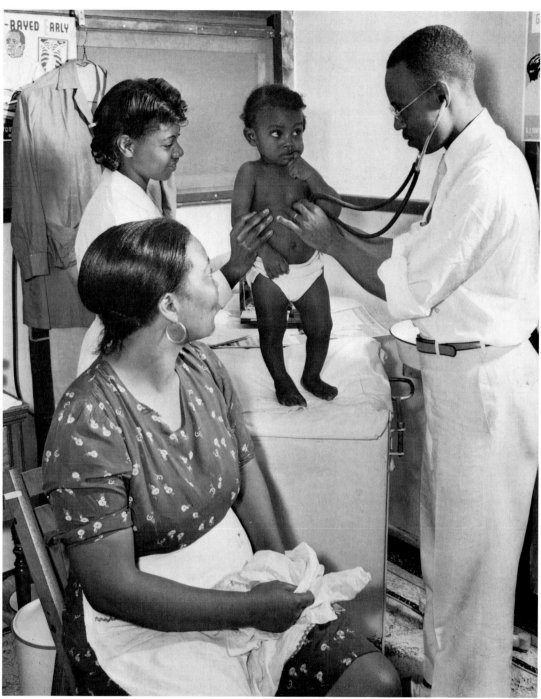

A doctor checks an infant's heartbeat. The effects of segregation were felt in Clarksville's medical community: When Wilma was growing up, there was only one doctor to attend all of the town's blacks.

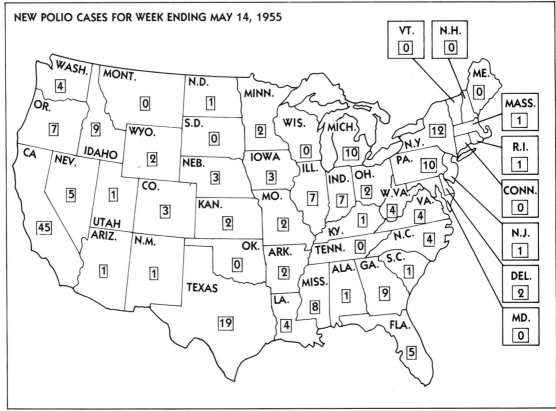

NEW POLIO CASES FOR WEEK ENDING MAY 14, 1955

Two decades after Wilma contracted polio in 1944, the crippling and often deadly disease continued to claim many new victims. This map depicts the number of outbreaks across the nation in a single week in 1955; polio vaccines were not perfected until the early 1960s.

fail to Meharry Medical College, 50 miles away, in Nashville, Tennessee. They would board the Greyhound bus hoping there were seats for them in the back, the only place blacks were allowed to sit. In her autobiography, Rudolph wrote, "What I remember best about those years of treatments is the bus rides. Always a Greyhound bus, always the same route, and always the people who were black sat in the back." Once in Nashville, Wilma had to undergo physical therapy—often pain-

ful exercise and massage sessions to strengthen her paralyzed leg. Then she and her mother rushed to catch a bus for the trip back to Clarksville.

Taxing as these treatments were, Wilma looked forward to the trips to Nashville. "I was getting out of Clarksville," she said, "I was seeing other things, even though it was the same things every time. I was traveling." Wilma saw homes, farms, and towns— an entire, vast world beyond the confines of her neighborhood. She daydreamed endlessly about what life must be like in the places she saw. Someday, she promised herself, she would experience firsthand what life had to offer outside Clarksville's city limits. First she would break out of the bonds of her leg brace, then she would cast off the additional bonds of being poor and black in a small southern town.

Meanwhile, Wilma's infirmity prevented her from sharing in the fun that most children take for granted. At the age of six, when her peers were skipping off to kindergarten, Wilma remained home, her useless leg strapped into a heavy metal brace. The long days spent confined at home took an inevitable toll. In her autobiography, Rudolph wrote that, "Being left behind had a terrible effect on me. I was so lonely, and I felt rejected. I would ... close my eyes, and just drift off into a sinking feeling, going down, down, down. I cried a lot."

But through those hard years, her family never gave up. They bolstered Wilma's confidence when all seemed hopeless; cheered her on as she struggled to regain use of her wasted limb; and saw her through the pain of her numerous setbacks during her recovery. Wilma also received the constant support of Dr. Coleman, Clarksville's only black doctor. As she later recalled, "He would come by the house every so often to check up on me; I remember

him to this day as being such a beautiful man. He was so kind and nice, and he never pressured the poor black people for money.... He would say, 'Wilma, everything is gonna turn out all right. You just fight this thing, you understand?' "

And so, finally, Wilma marshaled her strength and determination. She wrote in her autobiography:

> I remember I started getting mad about it all. I got angry. I went through the stage of asking myself, "Wilma, what is this existence all about? Is it about being sick all the time? It can't be." So I started getting angry about things, fighting back in a new way, with a vengeance. I think I started acquiring a competitive spirit right then and there, a spirit that would make me successful in sports later on. I was mad, and I was going to beat these illnesses no matter what. No more taking what comes, no more drifting off, no more wondering. Enough was enough.

Impressed with Wilma's dedication, the doctors in Nashville taught Mrs. Rudolph to put Wilma through the regimen at home. Many nights, Mrs. Rudolph, herself tired after a long day's work, would sit on Wilma's bed and massage her daughter's wasted leg well into the evening hours.

Wilma repaid her family for their help through her courage, her refusal to acknowledge pain, and her playful

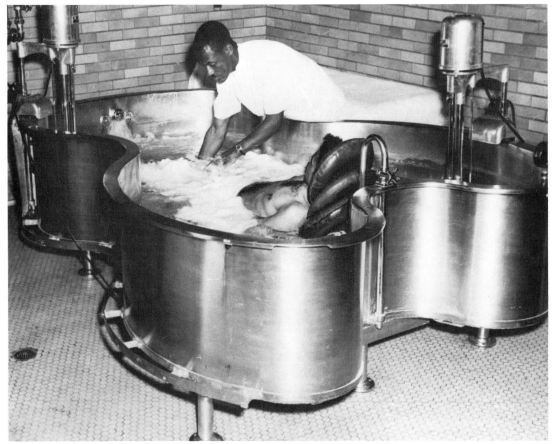

A student at Nashville's all-black Meharry Medical College massages a paralyzed patient's limbs. Wilma traveled to Meharry twice a week, where she underwent exercise and whirlpool sessions similar to the one shown here.

disposition. She joked in her autobiography that although her disability excused her from household chores, "I was sort of the house pet. I just moved around from one chair to another chair, and nagged and bugged everybody who was doing something. . . . It was like they were doing all the work, and I was doing all the entertaining. . . .

I never felt guilty because I felt I really did have a little role, and that was to keep the rest of them going. I was like a gimpy-legged cheerleader."

Wilma took her responsibilities as "cheerleader" very seriously and even pretended to be healthier than she actually was in order to encourage her parents and siblings. In the way some people learn to fake a limp, she carefully perfected a walk that looked as though her leg were stronger than it really was. Seeing her walk with a less noticeable limp, they believed that her progress was real, and their enthusiasm remained high.

When she was alone, however, Wilma would sometimes fall victim to bouts of depression. Recalling these times, Rudolph wrote, "I would get home at night and sneak off into an empty room, and I would study that leg all the time, study it to see if it was getting better. There had to be some visible improvement, I would tell myself, after all of this, there just had to be." Unfortunately, for several years, there was no significant improvement.

Because her weak leg made it difficult for Wilma to attend school, a tutor periodically came out to her home. The rest of the time her mother and older sisters and brothers filled in, helping her master the basics of math and reading. Finally, when Wilma was seven years old, she could walk steadily enough on her leg brace to enter the Cobb Elementary School. Rudolph recalls, "The first day I went into that school, I was terrified. I had been alone so much of my life that I was terrified of my own peer group, simply because I never spent that much time with kids my own age. I was aware, too, of the social judgments that kids made, like judging you on how much

Six-year-old Wilma Rudolph's polio-damaged left leg is evident in this photograph of her with her older sister Yvonne.

money your father made, what kind of clothes you wore, superficial things like that. It was intimidating to me, because I knew I was poor, moneywise, and I knew my clothes were made by my mother and not bought in some fancy store."

Wilma, who had long dreamed of

Wearing leg braces resembling the one Wilma wore, a polio-stricken teenager gazes at a portrait of U.S. president Franklin D. Roosevelt—himself a polio victim.

joining the other children at school, wanted desperately to be accepted by her classmates. When the other children made fun of Wilma's weak leg and cumbersome metal brace, her brothers and sisters lined up solidly to defend her. And Wilma herself responded to her antagonists by growing "determined to go beyond them, to do something someday that none of them would ever do, so then they'd have to accept me."

Hanging around the schoolyard, she watched her classmates at play, even though she was unable to participate. She took a keen interest in their games, dreaming of the day she could join them. Not a day went by when she and her family did not work to free her leg from the prison of that steel brace.

For all those years, until she was nearly 10, no one but her family and doctors ever saw her without her brace. It was a part of her in people's eyes—until one memorable Sunday.

As was true in so many small towns, the spiritual and social center of the black community was the local church. Virtually everyone who knew Wilma Rudolph was gathered in the church on that Sabbath, waiting for the service to begin. Suddenly, people sitting in the front of the church heard a buzz from the rear. They turned to see Wilma bravely walking down the aisle—on her own two legs, without the metal brace. As she made her way to her pew, Wilma's smile was brighter than a thousand-watt bulb.

But Wilma's victory was not total that day. For the next two years she wore the brace for support as she slowly recovered her full strength. Then came the momentous day when Mrs. Rudolph carefully wrapped the brace and mailed it back to the hospital in Nashville. According to Rudolph's autobiography, she felt as if she were embarking on a new beginning, "My whole life suddenly changed just as I was ending my sixth-grade year in school. No more brace; I was healthy all over my body for the first time."

Finally free of her leg brace when she was 12 years old, Wilma Rudolph threw herself into the games she had long watched from the sidelines—and quickly became a fine athlete.

THREE

The Basketball Star

In 1952, 12-year-old Wilma Rudolph finally achieved her dream of shedding her handicap and becoming like other children. Looking back on this time, Rudolph recalls, "I felt at that point that my life was beginning at last." Now she set her sights on her next goal: to become not just ordinary, but special.

Surprisingly, for someone who had spent years strapped in a leg brace, she decided she would make her mark on the basketball court. Basketball had always been a favorite pastime in Clarksville. An improvised hoop made from the rim of a bushel basket was enough to get a game going. Any old ball would do. The children of Clarksville could play for hours on end, seven days a week, year-round.

Wilma's brace had kept her out of the action, but she had spent countless hours watching others play. She stud-

ied every shot, pass, and rebound. She mentally catalogued each move that worked and analyzed every one that did not. Sitting on the sidelines, she had amassed a knowledge of the nuances of the game that was far superior to most other players her age.

All that remained, when she finally shed what she called her "convict's leg irons," was to work so that her body could catch up with her ambitions. Her mother tried to dissuade her from pursuing sports, worried that all the years of massage and therapy would be wasted if Wilma were injured. But Wilma could not be stopped any more than she had been defeated by polio.

So when she entered Burt High School, which Clarkville's black students attended from grades 7 through 12, basketball became the center of Wilma's life. The once-clumsy, skinny girl with the gimpy leg now discovered

Students gather on the steps of Burt High School, which Wilma attended from 7th through 12th grade. The school's gym was the scene of the first of her many athletic triumphs.

she could move with grace and style. Moreover, she was fast, and she was sure of her footing. To top her other advantages, she seemed to be growing taller every day.

Wilma's older sister, Yvonne, played on the school's girls' basketball team, and Wilma vowed to follow in her footsteps. She signed up for tryouts soon after entering Burt High. Knowing Wilma had worn a leg brace for the last six years, many coaches would have been too nervous about the possibility of her reinjuring herself to let her play. But to Wilma's great joy, Coach Clinton Gray took her on the team. She was not sure whether the coach had taken pity on her, sensed her determination, or simply given in to her sister's pleading. But whatever the reason, it did not matter to Wilma as long as her name was on the list of players who made the cut.

Given the opportunity to join the team, Wilma plunged in with characteristic determination. The years of rigorous physical therapy made it second nature for her to work long and hard at practices. It was as if she were making up for the times she could not run and play like other children.

Soon her skills had increased to the point that it became obvious to observers and teammates that she was very

Notre Dame University forward Tom Hawkins seems to defy gravity in this 1958 photograph. Basketball, the favorite sport in Clarksville, soon became an obsession with Wilma.

talented. Despite Wilma's abilities, Coach Gray virtually ignored her for three long seasons. Sometimes he did not have her suit up for games. Even when she was in uniform, she usually just sat on the bench, playing only in the final minutes of games if her team was far ahead or far behind. As she recalled, "I used to sit there on the bench and dream about someday becoming a star for this team, but the coach still didn't know I was alive."

Wilma, however, refused to grow disillusioned, to lose interest, or to waste the long hours she spent "warming the bench." She watched each move and every player, analyzing, planning. Between games, she practiced for several hours every day. Her persistence earned her a new nickname, "Skeeter" (slang for *mosquito*), because Coach Gray complained that she was "buzzing around like a 'skeeter' wherever I turn!" Finally, after three seasons of watching and waiting, she confronted Coach Gray. Wilma was direct and to the point: She asked for a spot on the starting team.

The coach listened but did not give her an answer. In fact, as the first game of the season approached, no one on the team knew who would be in the starting lineup. For Wilma, the tension was growing unbearable.

Finally, minutes before the start of the first game, all the girls lined up along the bench on their side of the

Black teenagers attempt to enter Little Rock's Central High School for the first time in 1957. Although the Supreme Court had declared segregated education unconstitutional in 1954, segregation continued in many schools, including Clarksville's Burt High.

gym. Coach Gray approached them with a mysterious smile. He did not say a word; he just strolled quietly past the assembled team. Five times he reached out to give a little tug to the sleeve of the girl he was passing. Five times those tugs let loose a whoop from the owner of the sleeve and cheers from the rest of the team. And this time, after three years, one of the sleeves—and one of the whoops—belonged to Wilma. She was in the starting lineup.

Coach Gray's tactics worked. His team was so fired up they would have taken on the Boston Celtics. They went on to trounce their opponents in that first game.

Morale continued to soar during the first key Middle East Tennessee Conference home game, and it seemed that the entire school population packed the bleachers to watch the contest. The game was also the first big test of the new sophomore starting guard—Wilma Rudolph.

Wilma quickly became the darling of the crowd. The sickly child who had worn a leg brace just two years before responded to her first crucial starting assignment by racking up 32 points. That season Wilma spurred her team to victory in the Middle East Tennessee Conference. Burt High not only had a new starter but also a new star.

Winning the conference title earned the team a spot in the state tournament, the Tennessee High School Girls' Championships, which were held in Nashville. Their supporters were nervous when Burt High drew another strong team in the lottery that decided their first-round opponents. But the players were confident, and their confidence proved justified when Wilma Rudolph tossed in 26 points to capture another triumph. Now the regional championship seemed almost within their grasp.

Their second-round opponents were a weaker team, and perhaps Burt's smugness turned into carelessness. According to Rudolph, "We had ourselves convinced we were going to win the whole thing and go down in history as being a real Cinderella team. But we turned into pumpkins instead."

The Burt High steamroller came to a crashing halt as Wilma's team was defeated by eight points in a game marred by sloppy ball handling and poor defense. Wilma was devastated and blamed herself for the loss, which eliminated the team from the tournament.

But out of that defeat would come

Once she had made the Burt High girls' basketball team, Wilma worked out at every opportunity. Her dedication, in addition to her innate ability, eventually made her a dominant athlete.

an opportunity Wilma barely could have imagined—the opportunity for this dirt-poor southern black girl to attend college and travel the globe as a world-class athlete, all expenses paid. On a day when Wilma's dreams of winning a state championship in basketball were crushed, the way was paved for new and more marvelous dreams to take their place.

Rudolph's life was changed forever when Tennessee State track coach Ed Temple spotted her talent while he was officiating a Burt High basketball game.

FOUR

The Making of a Champion

Ed Temple, who had presided over Burt High's defeat in the Tennessee High School Girls' Championships, worked as a referee mainly because the job enabled him to scout out new talent for his college team. As women's track coach at Tennessee State University in Nashville, he had transformed the school's team, the Tigerbelles, into a powerhouse, one of the top teams in the country.

Being discovered by Ed Temple was a major break for a young athlete. The track scholarships he offered made college educations possible for many young black women who could otherwise never afford to attend school on their own. The day he saw 10th grader Wilma Rudolph for the first time, even as a player on a losing team, he knew he had found a natural athlete. With her long, powerful legs and imposing height, she had the perfect sprinter's body.

By the time she was spotted by Coach Temple, Wilma had already gained some track experience. She had joined Burt's track team two years before, mostly as a way to keep busy between basketball seasons. The school's scanty athletic budget allowed for only a small, improvised women's track program. Basically, the girls just ran: When weather was good they raced outdoors; when it was bad they jogged around the halls of the school. Coach Gray volunteered his time, but he had no real experience coaching track.

From time to time the track team would drive to a nearby town to compete against girls from other schools. These meets, called "Playdays," were as informal as the training. Nobody

After turning in a poor performance at her first official track meet, held at Alabama's Tuskegee Institute, Rudolph realized that she could not rely on natural ability alone to win races.

worried much about documenting times or standings or records.

Despite the informality, one girl stood out—Wilma Rudolph. The tall, skinny ninth grader won every single race in which she competed. But she never thought much of this accomplishment; she was still preoccupied with basketball. Looking back, Rudolph recalls, "Running, at the time, was nothing but pure enjoyment for me. I was winning without really working."

In 1956, Wilma joined other young women from all over the South to participate in her first official track meet. The Amateur Athletic Union (AAU) contest was held at Alabama's Tuskegee Institute, the first college campus that Wilma or any of her teammates had ever seen. Rudolph remembers, "When we got to the track, these girls from Georgia really looked like runners, but I paid them no mind because, well, I was a little cocky. I did think I could wipe them out because, after all, I had won every single race I had ever been in up to that point." Her friends shared her enthusiasm; they planned a big victory celebration for her after the meet.

But Wilma's raw speed was no match for the vastly superior training and experience of the other girls; she lost every single race she entered. She was devastated at first, but the defeat taught her a lesson: "Winning is great, sure, but if you are really going to do

Ed Temple's program for promising young runners at Tennessee State covered all aspects of racing, from physical technique to mental preparation.

something in life, the secret is learning how to lose. Nobody goes undefeated all the time. If you can pick up after a crushing defeat, and go on to win again, you are going to be a champion someday." Wilma resolved that if natural talent was not enough, she would learn some techniques that would enable her to develop her potential.

To her surprise and great delight, later that year Ed Temple invited her to spend the summer living and training with other promising high-school students at Tennessee State University.

It was an incredible opportunity. As Wilma's mother told her, "You're the first one in this house that ever had the chance to go to college. If running's going to do that, I just want you to set your mind to be the best!"

The only hesitation Wilma had in accepting Temple's offer was that the summer at Tennessee State would interrupt her first romance. Her boyfriend was Robert Eldridge, a student at Burt High who was also a fine young athlete. Wilma and Robert had known each other since she first started at Cobb Elementary School. In her autobiography, Rudolph described their childish "courtship": "He was so mean, just a mean little kid, but I knew he liked me. I would be walking home from school, and he'd always be out there, every afternoon, and he'd throw rocks at me as a way of getting my attention.... He was a devil, but an all-right sort of devil, and I liked him."

In high school, they started dating; and aside from athletics, Robert became one of the most important fixtures in Wilma's life. But as much as she liked him, the chance to get real training proved too potent a lure for her to resist. Wilma went to Nashville with Coach Temple. She spent the summer working hard on critical elements of running that she had never thought about before—breathing, starts, and race strategy. She was placed on a training schedule that

built endurance while refining her natural speed. Wilma did exercises to increase her muscle tone, and she was lectured constantly about the mental toughness she needed to develop if she was to become a champion.

The mental aspect of running turned out to be the most challenging for Wilma. The small-town girl who had spent so many years silently observing the "big kids" found herself in awe of the college track stars with whom she was training. Even though she knew she was as fast as the other girls, she held back in races, letting the older runners win. She explained in her autobiography, "I thought if you're a high school kid, you don't go around showing up established stars by beating them."

Coach Temple pounded away at her attitude throughout the summer of 1956, encouraging her to gear up for the next AAU meet, to be held in Philadelphia, Pennsylvania, in late August. Wilma accepted his challenge. The meet was the first time she had ever been "up North." Rudolph remembered, "Everything in Philadelphia seemed so foreign to me; the buildings seemed so big, so awesome, I was intimidated. When we went to the stadium—Franklin Field—I nearly fainted. I had never seen a stadium that big before, and I actually felt like a midget."

Despite her anxieties, the six-foot-

Medalists Wilma Rudolph (left) and Joann Terry stand with Coach Temple following their team's sixth consecutive victory at national Amateur Athletic Union meets.

tall "midget" emerged victorious that day. She anchored the winning relay team and won the 75- and 100-yard dashes. And then, at a press conference following the contest, she received a special honor—the chance to

Jackie Robinson, the first black to play major league baseball, stands at bat. When he met Rudolph in 1956, he advised the awestruck teenager to continue racing, no matter what the obstacles.

meet baseball superstar Jackie Robinson.

Robinson was perhaps the most admired black athlete in America at the time. In 1947, he had become the first black to play major league baseball. He had fought a tremendous battle against racial bigotry and won. His struggle had won him a place in history, and his fine, aggressive play earned him a spot in the Baseball Hall of Fame in 1962.

Wilma and a few of her teammates were asked to pose with Robinson for photographs. She was thrilled—but she was absolutely stunned when Robinson actually spoke to her. His gentle questions and genuine interest made a lasting impression on the awestruck 16 year old. Years later she wrote, "For the first time in my life I had a black person I could look up to as a real hero." She would always treasure Robinson's advice: "You are a fascinating runner," he told her. "Don't let anything, or anybody, keep you from running."

Wilma's confidence was at an all-time high. She did not even hesitate when Coach Ed Temple invited her to travel with his Tennessee State team to the tryouts for the 1956 Olympic Games.

The word *Olympics* had meant little to Wilma until Temple suggested she attempt to make the team. She had assumed the games were just another big track meet. She was amazed to

An athlete uses a torch to set the Olympic symbol ablaze. Before Rudolph left for Melbourne, she knew very little about the history and traditions of the world's most spectacular and prestigious athletic competition.

learn the Olympics drew athletes from all over the globe—*and* that the 1956 contest would be held in Melbourne, Australia. Sixteen-year-old Wilma Rudolph had barely spent any time away from her home in Clarksville. She was excited and more than a little intimidated by the prospect of traveling to an exotic locale to participate in an international competition.

Rudolph (left) and Olympic veteran Mae Faggs break the tape simultaneously in this photo finish from the 200-meter race that earned both women a spot on the 1956 U.S. Olympic team.

Just a few weeks after her triumph in Philadelphia, Wilma was driven across the country to the Olympic tryouts in Seattle, Washington. With her were some older girls from Tennessee State, including Mae Faggs, a U.S. record holder and a two-time veteran of the Olympics. Faggs took Rudolph under her wing, talking with her constantly to improve her confidence. In her autobiography, Rudolph wrote that Faggs "always seemed to be telling me, without really coming out with it in so many words, that the time to start performing as an individual was now and to stop worrying about fitting in with everybody else, stop worrying about whether or not so-and-so is still going to like me if I win that race. . . . At first, I wondered what she was talking about, but then it started sinking in— performing as an individual. An *individual*."

Faggs's advice was hard for Wilma to remember during the pressures of the Olympic trials. Wilma was so nervous she could not eat, and she constantly felt as if she were on the verge of getting sick. Before the qualifying heat in the 200-meter dash, Faggs, who was also running in the race, told Wilma, "Put everything out of your mind and concentrate on doing nothing else but sticking with me."

Wilma did what her friend told her. She got off to a good start, and to her surprise she found herself passing the Olympic champion. Faggs came back

The high-spirited U.S. women's Olympic track-and-field team assembled for this photograph shortly before their departure for Melbourne, Australia. Rudolph is second from the left in the second row.

at her, and the two runners hit the tape that marked the finish line in a dead heat (a tie). Immediately, Faggs ran up and hugged Wilma. Both women had made the U.S. Olympic team.

"From that moment on," Rudolph recalled in her autobiography, "it seemed as if I wasn't afraid to challenge anybody anywhere. Whatever fears I had, fears of offending somebody else by beating them, fears of being rejected by my teammates if I did too well, all of those fears vanished." Wilma Rudolph, the youngest member of the U.S. team, was ready to represent her country at the 1956 Olympics.

As a child, Rudolph had been thrilled by her bus trips to Nashville for physical therapy; in 1956, she traveled to Australia to race against the fastest runners in the world.

FIVE

The Melbourne Olympics

Sixteen-year-old Wilma Rudolph returned home from Seattle a celebrity. Everyone wanted to congratulate Clarksville's homegrown Olympic contender. But Rudolph's fame had not relieved her financial problems. Knowing her father and mother did not have very much money, a group of merchants gave her a new wardrobe and brand-new luggage to take to Melbourne. Years later, Rudolph remembered the generosity of the people of Clarksville: "I love them dearly for the help they gave me when I most needed it." The townspeople even organized a joyous send-off ceremony when she left for Los Angeles to start her Olympic training.

The flight to the West Coast was Rudolph's first plane ride. Her primary memory of the trip was turning down the stewardess's offer of food because she thought she would have to pay for the meal. Even after Mae Faggs whispered to her that the food was free, Rudolph was too nervous to eat.

Once in Los Angeles, however, she began to relax. The older members of the team adopted her as a kid sister. As Rudolph felt increasingly comfortable, she began to run very well. She was particularly happy that Ed Temple was also in Los Angeles, assisting the U.S. team's track coach, Nel Jackson. Because Coach Jackson was just getting acquainted with the strengths and weaknesses of the individual runners on her team, Temple's day-to-day guidance was invaluable.

During this time, Mae Faggs continued to give Rudolph the benefit of her experience. She told the eager high-school student that the five interlocking rings of the Olympic symbol stood

Coach Ed Temple, surrounded by the Melbourne-bound Tennessee State team, flashes a "V-for-Victory" sign. Rudolph is on the far left.

for five continents (North America, South America, Europe, Africa, and Asia) linked together in friendly competition. Faggs gave her tips on running, both individually and as part of a relay team. She also continued to boost Rudolph's confidence, aware that the teenager's state of mind—her will to win—might very well be the crucial

factor in her performance in Melbourne.

Finally, training camp was over, and the team boarded an airplane for the two-day journey to Australia. The first stop was Honolulu, Hawaii. During the stopover, Rudolph and two other women on the team, both of whom were also black southerners, went win-

Rudolph (front right) dines at the Olympic Village. Initially overwhelmed by the international atmosphere of the games, she finally realized that all the athletes were there for the same reasons: "To win and to meet new people."

dow shopping in town. When a white woman walking her dog saw the three black women approaching, she gave them a horrified look and hurriedly crossed the street. This stark display of prejudice saddened Rudolph. She and her teammates would compete in the Olympics to honor the entire United States—yet to this white American, they were contemptible.

The thought depressed her until the airplane landed in the Fiji Islands. Rudolph was amazed to find that the majority of the islanders were not white. Dark-skinned men and women were not a hated minority here, as they

This aerial photograph of the Olympic park in Melbourne, Australia, affords a view of the sites for several of the events.

often were in the United States. They ran the entire country, sharing a language and culture all their own. Now Wilma recalled that Mae Faggs once claimed to treasure her travels, her knowledge of the world, as much as her Olympic medals. Wilma was now seeing some of those marvels for herself.

From the Fijis, the team flew on to Melbourne, where they were housed in a special Olympic compound built just for the competitors. Rudolph found that the athletes were wonderfully curious about each others' countries, habits, life-styles, and languages. They spent endless hours comparing notes, exchanging mementos and souvenirs, and communicating with and without the benefit of common languages. For the first time in her life, Rudolph felt that no one cared that she was black. The only judgments made about men and women in the Olympics were determined by stopwatches, time clocks, and measuring tapes.

Another new experience for Rudolph was being asked for her autograph. She and the other women on the U.S. team were so flattered by the attention of the fans that they spent an hour a day outside the Olympic Village, signing autographs and just getting to know the Australians. The exotic scenery and even the climate were thrilling—although it was November,

Australia—which is in the Southern Hemisphere, where the seasons are reversed—was warm.

But the prospect of actually *competing* in the games, against the world's finest athletes, was making Wilma anxious. For one thing, her training was not going well. She and the other women from Tennessee State missed the knowledge and encouragement of Ed Temple, who had been unable to travel with the team. "He gave us this feeling of security, just being around," Rudolph recalled later. "So there was an empty spot for us, but none of us were admitting it, even though we all felt it."

Rudolph faced her first test on the third day of the Olympics in the women's 200-meter dash. She was so nervous and so serious about her concentration that later she could not remember the name of a single runner she competed against nor any details of the race. Despite her trepidation, she scored a third-place finish in the qualifying race—on sheer speed alone. Now the gangling, 6-foot, 89-pound runner moved on to the semifinals.

The semifinal race, held the next day, proved an even tougher challenge. Again, she finished third—but this time only the first- and second-place runners advanced to the finals. She was eliminated from competition. In her autobiography, Rudolph described her desolation, "I felt terrible.... I

couldn't eat or sleep. I felt as if I had let down everybody back home and the whole United States of America."

Three days after her defeat, however, she forced herself to return to the Olympic Stadium. There she was inspired by the example of the great Australian runner Betty Cuthbert. Only 18 years old, Cuthbert was undeniably the star of women's track. She was also very friendly and had gone out of her way to talk with Rudolph. She had even shown the American runners where they could buy special Australian track shoes, which were unusually light because they were made out of kangaroo leather.

Rudolph, however, did not have the $20 for the shoes, though as she later recalled, she "wanted them desperately." Mae Faggs offered to lend her the money, but Wilma refused. She knew that her parents could not afford to pay Faggs back.

Now, watching Cuthbert sweep the women's 100- and 200-meter dashes, Rudolph's flagging spirits revived. She told herself, "You've got four years to get there yourself, but you've got to

Australian sprinter Betty Cuthbert (third from left) races toward victory in the 1956 women's 100-meter final. Cuthbert's success inspired Rudolph, who was downcast after her failure to qualify for the 200-meter race.

Team captain Mae Faggs (right) uses Rudolph's leg to illustrate a point as she gives her fellow members of the U.S. track team advice on competing in the 1956 Olympics.

work hard for those four years and pay the price."

She had one more chance to redeem herself in the current games—the women's 400-meter relay race. The relay was a grueling test of reflexes as well as of speed because of the split-second timing necessary to seize the baton. A misstep or a tiny misjudgment could cost the team the race.

Indeed, baton passing had pro-

duced big upsets in previous Olympic Games. In the 1936 Olympics, the same contest in which Jesse Owens led the U.S. men's track team to victory, the German women's team had been overwhelmingly favored to win the relay. In the finals, the third German runner, Marie Dollinger, led the race by a commanding eight yards when she handed off to her anchor runner, Ilse Dorffeldt. Dorffeldt, however, dropped the baton. As the Nazi leadership watched in dismay, the German team was disqualified, and the Americans won the gold medal.

History had repeated itself in the 1952 Olympics. The favored Australian women's team had set a new world record by running the relay race in 46.1 seconds during the qualifying heats. Then, in the finals, the third runner bumped into the anchor during the handoff, and the anchor runner dropped the baton. The Australians managed to stay in the race, but they lost enough time to finish fifth. Once again, the U.S. team won the gold medal.

Rudolph and her teammates—Mae Faggs, Margaret Matthews, and Isabelle Daniels—were having trouble with their baton passing in practice. They could not seem to get their timing right, and they were afraid that the problem would only get worse under the intense pressure of the Olympic competition. On the day of the race,

The members of the 1936 U.S. women's track-and-field team wave to their fans. The American relay racers pulled off an upset after the favored Germans dropped the baton in the final race. In the 1960 Olympics, history nearly repeated itself—although this time it was the U.S. team that nearly lost the gold medal due to a faulty handoff.

the entire team was nervous until Mae Faggs called them together. A veteran of international competition, she motivated her teammates with a pep talk, saying, "Let's go get 'em. Let's give it all we've got, let's make it into the top three and win ourselves a medal."

When the race started, Faggs got off to a good start and ran an excellent first leg, keeping the Americans tied for the lead. Although Matthews, the second U.S. runner, had won third place in both the 100- and 200-meter dashes, she lost ground to several teams on the second leg before handing off to Rudolph. Fortunately, the handoff was excellent, and Rudolph ran a superb leg, pulling her team into third place before passing off to Daniels. Daniels not only clung to third position but

Avery Brundage, president of the International Olympic Committee, makes his closing speech on the last day of the Melbourne competition. As she left the 1956 games, Rudolph vowed that she would compete again in 1960.

almost caught the second-place team. Against all odds, the American runners had captured a medal. The U.S. women's 400-meter relay team had beaten such favored teams as the Soviets and East Germans and had finished third behind the winning Australians and the second-place British. Along with her teammates, 16-year-old Wilma Rudolph had won an Olympic bronze medal, the third-place prize.

Rudolph still regretted her loss in the women's 100-meter dash, but she was thrilled by the team's success. As she later wrote, "I was happy that I salvaged something out of Melbourne, and a bronze medal still isn't all that bad for a high school kid from Tennessee." But more than anything else, the Melbourne Olympics had given Rudolph a new resolve that would propel her to future accomplishments. She left Australia bent on a goal: to return to the games four years later, and this time, to win not bronze medals but gold.

Returning Olympian Wilma Rudolph (second from left) is greeted by her mother, father, and younger sister, Charlene.

When she arrived home in Clarksville, she found that Burt High School had been closed for the day so that the students could attend a special ceremony in her honor. An embarrassed Rudolph was cheered and showered with bouquets. Then she was called upon to make a speech, an experience that she said "scared me more than the Olympics had."

All this attention did not go to Rudolph's head. When she learned that the first basketball game of the season was scheduled for that very night she sought out Coach Gray. "I've been doing more running than basketball playing, but I'll tell you something, Coach Gray, I am in great shape. . . .can I play tonight? Please?"

He said yes. And despite the jet lag she suffered from her three-day trip halfway around the world, despite her new status as an international celebrity, Wilma Rudolph suited up that evening and played high-school basketball with all her old enthusiasm.

67

After the Melbourne Olympics, Rudolph tried to return to her previous life of basketball games, track meets, and high-school social events. Yet she often found that her classmates treated her more like a celebrity than a peer.

Hard Times

Wilma Rudolph, now a high-school junior, vowed that her celebrity as an Olympic champion would not change her or her life. But, inevitably, it did. Although her fellow students and the teachers at Burt High soon stopped treating her as a star, they could not help feeling that she was special. Players on opposing basketball teams treated Rudolph with an awe that made her uncomfortable. When track season came around, she found that runners who had always been stiff competition now looked upon her as unbeatable and ran halfheartedly as a result. This lack of competition frustrated her, but she understood the reasons—after all, she herself had been intimidated when she first faced the seemingly invincible college track stars at Tennessee State.

The most painful evidence that she was considered somehow different emerged at the Tennessee High School Girls' (basketball) Championship. Rudolph's fine ball handling and accurate shooting helped propel the Burt High team into the tournament, but in the final seconds of the big game, she lost the ball to their opponents. Luckily, the other team failed to capitalize on her error, and soon the gym was filled with the joyous cheers of Burt's fans. But Rudolph remembers Coach Gray's voice rising above the others: "That was a stupid thing to do," he shouted at her, "throw the ball away like that. How can you be so stupid?" A hush fell over the gym, and humiliated, Rudolph fled to the locker room, asking herself, "Why's he always trying to make an example out of me by picking on me all the time?"

Off the court and the track, she

This aerial photograph of Burt High shows the track where Rudolph did her early training. Pregnant for much of her senior year, Rudolph missed both the basketball and track seasons, but she finished her studies.

looked forward to brighter moments—especially to attending the Junior-Senior Prom. A friend had lent her a deep-blue formal dress, and her boyfriend, Robert Eldridge, presented her with a beautiful white orchid corsage. The excited couple arrived at the festivities in style, driving up in a brand-new, two-tone Ford borrowed from Eldridge's father. It was a wonderful night, too magical to end when the band had played its final song. So Rudolph and Eldridge and their friends piled into cars for a drive to Hopkinsville, Kentucky, just over the state line, where there was a nightclub that would admit teenagers under the legal drinking age. In the wee hours of the morning, the promgoers finally left the bar.

They were all in high spirits, and the highway was deserted, so someone suggested racing home to Clarksville. The following morning Rudolph was awakened by a frantic telephone call from Coach Gray. She was surprised at the relief in his voice when she answered—and then shocked to learn that one of the cars had never made it back. There had been a bad accident, claiming the life of Nancy Bowen, Rudolph's closest female friend.

The loss was devastating for Rudolph. As she later recalled, "Nancy's death was my first experience with tragedy. I couldn't handle it. I was an emotional wreck for weeks."

That summer, she returned to Tennessee State to continue her training with Coach Temple. He understood that her concentration had been shaken by the death of her friend, and he treated her gently. "Slowly, I started coming out of it," Rudolph recalled in her autobiography. "Being in another city, in another atmosphere, helped me do it."

The following fall, the beginning of her senior year in high school, Rudolph drew closer to Robert Eldridge, her date from the ill-fated prom. And then one day, during a routine physical, Rudolph found out that she was pregnant.

"I was mortified," she recalled in her autobiography. "Pregnant? I couldn't understand it. Robert and I had just started to get involved in sex, and here I was pregnant. We were both innocent about sex, didn't know anything about birth control or about contraceptives, but neither one of us ever thought it would result in this."

Indeed, 30 years ago, there were very few references to sex on television or on the radio and very little discussion of the subject in popular magazines or newspapers. Virtually no school systems had sex education programs. Most teenagers who did not get accurate information from their parents had no source of guidance at all.

The problem was especially difficult for a young woman such as Rudolph, who was raised in a very religious household. For her family, the Baptist faith was both a bridge and a wall. Her mother's deep, abiding trust in God provided the foundation for Rudolph's miraculous recovery from polio. Rudolph herself had wholeheartedly embraced religion at an early age, and that commitment had strengthened and comforted her during the long years of rehabilitation. The church also provided her with a community of loving friends. At the same time, the church's very strict moral stand made it difficult for Rudolph to discuss sex with her mother. "I couldn't ask about such things as sex, because sex was a taboo subject in the religion. A lot of

These Southern Baptist churchgoers accompany their hymns with handclaps and tambourines. The Rudolphs' strict Baptist faith made it difficult for Wilma to discuss sex with her mother.

things I wanted to know more about back then, and I should have been able to go to my mother for the answers." Instead, Rudolph found out the hardest possible way: by becoming pregnant when she was just 17.

Rudolph's options as a black teenager in a small southern town in the late 1950s were very limited. Abortion was illegal, and in the black community of Clarksville, "Nobody was sent away to live with an aunt for a while [to have the baby in secrecy before giving it up for adoption] like the white girls did." Rudolph's only alternative was to have the baby, then seek help from her family in caring for it.

When Mr. Rudolph heard that Wilma was expecting a child, he told his daughter two things. First, she was forbidden to see Eldridge, whom he blamed for his daughter's pregnancy. And secondly, as Rudolph reported in her autobiography, he told her, "Don't worry about anything, don't be ashamed of anything, everybody makes mistakes."

Rudolph's "mistake" threatened to cut short her future both as a student and as an athlete. But with the understanding of Coach Temple and her family, she was able to carry out her plans to finish school and to continue running track. Temple told her he would waive his standing rule against allowing mothers in his training program at Tennessee State. The problem

of caring for the baby was solved when Wilma's older sister, Yvonne, who had married and moved to St. Louis, agreed to take the child into her household until Wilma could care for a family full-time. "The people I loved were sticking by me," Rudolph recalled, "and that alone took a lot of pressure, and pain, and guilt, off my shoulders."

So Rudolph finished out her senior year in high school, graduating in June 1958. A month later she gave birth to a baby girl, whom she named Yolanda.

That September, Rudolph entered Tennessee State College on a full athletic scholarship. She found the adjustment to college very difficult. Coach Temple required that every woman in his program maintain a B average, and Rudolph had been accustomed to cutting classes in order to get in extra running time. Now she realized that she had to buckle down and spend more time on schoolwork. Because studying and training were so time-consuming, Temple discouraged any other activities, including social life.

This restriction was especially hard on Rudolph because, unlike the other young women on the track team, her "social life" centered around her baby. Yolanda was now living with the Rudolphs in Clarksville because Wilma had missed her so terribly when she was in St. Louis. As a mother, she had more responsibilities than her teammates, but Temple refused to give her

Coach Ed Temple stands between two Tennessee State track stars who proudly display their letter sweaters. Rudolph was thrilled when she finally became a Tigerbelle in 1958.

special treatment. Determined not to allow motherhood to interfere with her education and training, she accepted Coach Temple's discipline and learned to juggle her different roles. Rudolph worried more about being accepted as a Tennessee State Tigerbelle than she had about making the U.S. Olympic team. After all, the Olympics were held only once every four years, but college track was a daily activity. Then, too, she could not forget

that, just a few years earlier, she had been defeated time and again by the highly trained Tennessee State women.

Rudolph made the team her freshman year. But at the beginning of her crucial sophomore year, the year of the trials for the 1960 Olympic Games, she began to lose races regularly to her three other Tigerbelle teammates. Rudolph was near despair, especially because Coach Temple could not find any flaws in her technique. Finally, the

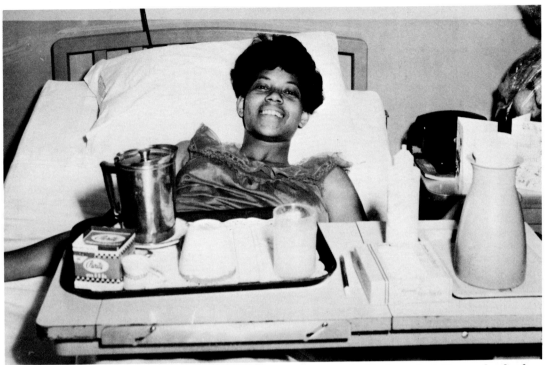

Rudolph recovers from her 1959 tonsillectomy in a Nashville hospital. Once she had beaten the tonsil infection that had been sapping her strength, she was ready to train for her second Olympics.

team doctor discovered the answer: A persistent tonsil infection had been sapping her strength. After she had her tonsils removed, Rudolph soon regained her position as the fastest of the Tigerbelles.

The recovery from tonsillitis marked the end of the difficult times Rudolph had suffered since the night of her junior prom. In August 1960, she won the 100- and 200-meter dashes at the Olympic trials, securing a place on the U.S. team. Better still, three of her fellow Tigerbelles would join her, forming a disciplined, well-coordinated team for the Olympic 400-meter relay race.

The best news of all came when Ed Temple, Rudolph's mentor, was named coach of the U.S. Olympic women's track team. It would give her the boost she had missed so desperately in Melbourne—the strong support of her own familiar trainer. Wilma Rudolph set her sights on Rome, host to the 1960 Olympic Games—where it seemed that her goal of winning three gold medals was almost within her grasp.

Wilma "Skeeter" Rudolph suits up for the Olympic Games in Rome. She came to her second Olympics armed with the confidence and maturity she had lacked in the 1956 contest.

SEVEN

Triumph in Rome

The U.S. Olympic team arrived in Rome well ahead of schedule, so they would have plenty of time to work out. The temperature hovered at the 100-degree mark, which severely hampered some of the athletes from northern countries. But for Rudolph and the Tigerbelles, the climate was comfortable—no worse than the Tennessee summers they were used to. The advantages seemed to be stacking up on their side.

But then, the Tuesday before the competition began, Rudolph suffered an injury. She was jogging across a field when she hit a small depression and fell, her ankle popping.

Would she be able to compete? The team doctor could not say. Her ankle seemed to be strained, not sprained or broken. He told her to keep off it for a few days.

Crushed at the prospect of missing her big chance, Rudolph followed his orders strictly. To keep her mind off her injury, she renewed her old friendships from Melbourne, met the new competitors, and as always, signed autographs for young fans.

Fortunately her injury responded to the rest, and she was well enough to compete in the 100- and 200-meter dashes. Both of them were run on straight, smooth tracks that put minimal strain on her ankle. She easily won her first qualifying heat in the 100-meter dash.

After her victory, she was so relaxed that when she stretched out on the infield to rest, she fell asleep. Her calmness stunned her fellow competitors.

Then came the second heat, when Rudolph really proved that she was a contender to be reckoned with. She

Rudolph shares the spotlight with second-place finisher Dorothy Hyman after the 100-meter dash, in which Rudolph won her first gold medal.

seemed to fly down the straightaway, tying the world record of 11.3 seconds held by Australian Shirley Strickland. By the finals, Rudolph's speed and grace had already made her a favorite of the Rome crowd, and they cheered wildly when she flew to victory in the finals of the 100-meter dash in an astounding 11.0 seconds.

It was a world-record time for the 100-meter dash—or would have been. Unfortunately, during the race, the wind behind Rudolph was blowing at 2.752 meters per second, just a little faster than the accepted standard of 2.0 meters per second. Because of the strong following wind, her time was disqualified for a world record.

The next competition was the 200-meter dash, and again Rudolph was

The "Tennessee Tigerbelles," the U.S. women's relay team, received international acclaim following their first-place finish in the 1960 Olympics. Standing from left to right are Rudolph, Lucinda Williams, Barbara Jones, and Martha Hudson.

the odds-on favorite. She was delighted when she won the first heat in an Olympic record time of 23.2 seconds. In the finals, her time was slower—24.0 seconds, but still fast enough to easily defeat Jutta Heine of Germany, her most formidable competitor. And fast enough to earn Rudolph her second gold medal.

With the attention of the entire world now focused on Rudolph, the Tigerbelles pushed on to the 400-meter relay. The four women responded to the pressure by setting a new world-record time in the qualifying heats. Joining them in the final were teams from Germany, Italy, the Soviet Union, Great Britain, and Poland. Rudolph's major concern about the final was her ankle—running on the curved relay track taxed its strength, and it hurt from the arduous qualifying heats. Then, too, there was always the fear that one of the Tigerbelles would drop the baton.

The first 2 U.S. runners gave the team a 2-yard lead at the 200-meter mark. Ironically, Germany's third runner was Brunhilde Hendrix. Her mother, Marie Dollinger, had been the third runner on the German 400-meter relay team in 1936—the year of Jesse Owens's triumph. It was Dollinger who

Rudolph crosses the finish line to win the women's 200-meter dash and her second gold medal.

81

had made the bad handoff to the anchor in the finals, losing the race and shaming Germany's arrogant leader, Adolf Hitler. For her daughter, however, there would be no fumbling: Hendrix handed off successfully to Jutta Heine.

Instead it would be Rudolph who fumbled, bobbling the handoff from Lucinda Williams and nearly dropping the baton. By the time she recovered, Jutta Heine and Russia's Irina Press had taken over the lead. But then, with a spectacular burst of speed, Rudolph pulled abreast of her competitors, passed them, and exploded across the finish line three-tenths of a second ahead of Press. The Tigerbelles were the jubilant victors—and Rudolph had won her third gold medal.

Rudolph described the first sweet moments of triumph in her autobiography:

> The feeling of accomplishment welled up inside me . . . three Olympic gold medals. I knew that was something nobody could ever take away from me, ever. After the playing of "The Star-Spangled Banner," I came away from the victory stand and I was mobbed. People were jumping all over me, pushing microphones into my face, pounding my back. I couldn't believe it. Finally the American officials grabbed me and escorted me to safety. One of them said, "Wilma, life will never be the same for you again." He was so right.

Rudolph was now the darling of the world press. Requests flooded in for photo sessions, interviews—for any word at all from the young black runner who was now established as the fastest woman in the world. The Italians nicknamed her "La Gazzella Nera," (The Black Gazelle); to the French she was "La Perle Noire" (The Black Pearl). In response to an overwhelming demand, Coach Temple hurriedly accepted invitations for Rudolph and her teammates to race in such European cities as Athens, Amsterdam, London, Cologne, and Berlin.

Before they left, the Tigerbelles were even invited to the Vatican to meet Pope John XXIII. The splendid architecture and artworks of the Vatican left the Americans so intimidated that they found themselves unconsciously talking in whispers, but the Pope put the awestruck athletes at ease. Rudolph wrote later that the Holy Father was "a real jolly fellow. He had rosy cheeks and he laughed a lot. He was a very happy man, and it was obvious that everybody around him loved him."

After the closing ceremonies in Rome, the Tigerbelles flew to England for the British Empire Games. There, once again, Wilma won the 100-meter dash. But by now, all the attention showered on Rudolph was beginning to make her teammates jealous. So great was the clamor over Rudolph, the other Tigerbelles began to feel that they were in her shadow. The longer

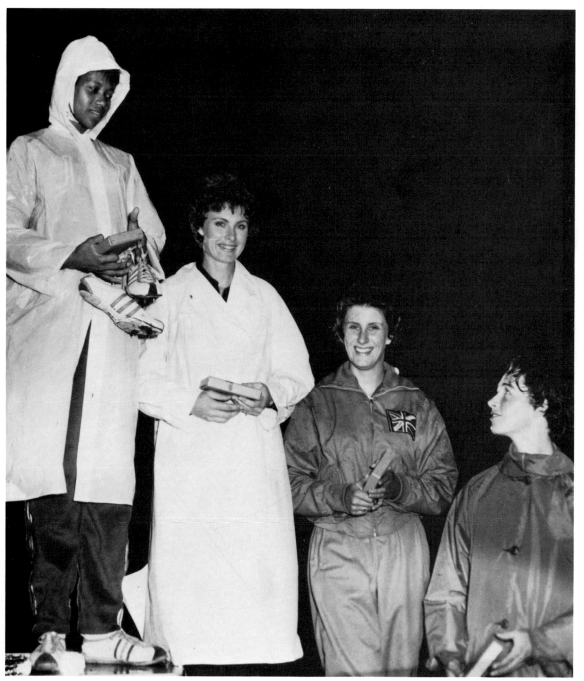

Rudolph hides her disheveled hair under a hood after her victory in the 100-meter dash at the British Empire Games. Envious of her fame, her fellow Tigerbelles had hidden her rollers before the awards ceremony.

people waited in line to meet Rudolph, the greater the distance her teammates felt from her. Because all four of them had shared in the Olympic triumph, they thought they deserved at least some of the adulation. Soon tensions grew so fierce that two of the Tigerbelles stopped speaking to Rudolph altogether.

The conflict came to a head during the Empire Games. One night, before a banquet, Rudolph needed to set her hair, which was wild from the humid English weather. "The fog and rain rolled in early," she recalled, "and all I could think of was Jack the Ripper." But the four Tigerbelles shared a single set of curlers—which was nowhere to be found. "I was running around looking for the curlers," Rudolph said, "and the other girls were pretending they had no idea whatsoever where the curlers were. I went to the banquet with my hair an absolute mess and Coach Temple blew his top."

Temple immediately held a team meeting and demanded an explanation. He called the malicious behavior of the other girls in hiding the curlers "stupid," and he ordered them to put their jealousy aside.

Temple's lecture did no good. The next day, the women were entered in the 440-yard relay. Rudolph's teammates decided they would not run very hard, so that the crowd packed into the stadium to see the "world's fastest woman" would be disappointed. Rudolph remembered, "They barely struggled along. By the time I got the baton, one girl was actually forty yards ahead of me with only 110 yards to go. Well, I was determined to win that race, because sometime in the middle of it I realized what was happening. So I poured it on like never before, ran the fastest anchor leg of my life, and caught up with her at the tape to win. I closed forty yards and actually pulled out the race. The crowd went crazy."

Wilma Rudolph received a standing ovation; the other three Tigerbelles received another scolding from Coach Temple. He told them that when they got back to Tennessee State, they would be put on probation. From then on, Rudolph's teammates performed up to their abilities on the track, but they still shunned her when the meets were over.

Rudolph continued to be the center of public attention for the rest of the tour. In Berlin, the German city where her hero Jesse Owens had been heckled by racist crowds 24 years before, she nearly caused a riot. But instead of the insults hurled at Owens, she was greeted with cheers. One fan became so carried away that he actually stole the shoes off her feet to keep as souvenirs. Maintaining the cool that characterized her performance at the Olympics, she responded gracefully to

A beaming Rudolph, joined by Ed Temple (left) and another Olympic athlete, waves to an adoring crowd. Her triumph in Rome made her an international celebrity.

even the most overzealous fans. Rudolph later credited her attitude to her upbringing, "I was never rude to the people who wanted to meet me or to the reporters who wanted interviews. I was taught that at home."

Although she enjoyed the outpouring of affection she received nearly everywhere she went, Rudolph was overjoyed when the tour came to an end and it was time to return to the United States. For all the excitement, for all the applause and acclaim, she was just plain homesick for Tennessee.

Rudolph holds a photograph of herself crossing a finish line at the 1960 Olympics. Decades later, she is still devoted to excellence in sports and uses her experience to inspire young athletes.

EIGHT

New Beginnings

When the exhausted U.S. women's track team stepped off the plane in Nashville, they found that an immense crowd had turned out to greet them. Rudolph later commented, "Everybody was there, it seemed—mayors of cities, the governor, judges, television stations, marching bands from the Tennessee State campus." There was the usual forest of television and radio microphones, and a jostling crowd of reporters and photographers clamored for Rudolph. By now, she was deft at handling questions and speaking in public, and her remarks delighted the crowd.

When the welcoming ceremonies ended, Coach Temple and his wife insisted that Rudolph stay with them in Nashville for a few days because the town of Clarksville needed some extra time to prepare for its own homecoming celebration. But the thought of waiting a few more days to see her family was too much for Rudolph to stand. That night, when the Temples thought she was asleep, she sneaked out of the house. She talked a friend into giving her a ride back to Clarksville, where she had a joyful midnight reunion with her mother and father. As she recounted in her autobiography, "I was back the next morning as if nothing had happened. That's running!"

Two days later, a police motorcade escorted Wilma Rudolph, the pride of Clarksville, back home for her victory party. Just outside town, the procession was joined by Rudolph's parents and daughter, Yolanda, now two years old. Parachutists from nearby Fort Campbell, Kentucky, staged a special jump in Rudolph's honor. But the most impressive part of the spectacle was the crowd that thronged the streets, cheering and waving banners. Amazingly, the entire town—black and white—turned out to greet her. As Rudolph later wrote, the parade "actually was the first integrated event in the history of the town. So was the banquet they gave for me that night; it was the first time in Clarksville's history that blacks and whites had gathered under the same roof for the same event. That's why it took so long to organize everything."

Rudolph's spectacular achievements had brought the people of Clarksville together. County Judge William Hudson told the 1,100 people who had crowded into the armory for the banquet, "Wilma has competed with the world and brought home three gold medals." Commenting on the integrated crowd, he noted that, "If you want to get good music out of a piano you have to play both white and black keys."

A few days later Rudolph was on the road again, this time on a national tour organized by the alumni of Tennessee State. In Chicago, Mayor Daley presented her with the key to the city. In New York City, the National Association for the Advancement of Colored People (NAACP) hosted a gala banquet where civil rights leader Roy Wilkins paid tribute to Rudolph's skill and determination. She attended a dizzy-

ing round of parties in Washington, D.C., where, as she later recalled, she "met ambassadors of countries I never knew existed."

By the beginning of 1961, Rudolph had received many of the world's most prestigious athletic awards. The Associated Press named her Woman Athlete of the Year. She became the first American to win Italy's Christopher Columbus award as the most outstanding international sports personality. A group of European sportswriters even named her "Sportsman of the Year," making her the first *woman* ever to win that title.

Amid all the hoopla, Rudolph returned to Tennessee State to finish her degree in elementary education. She also took a part-time job working at the university post office, and she hoped to spend more time with her family. But honors and invitations continued to stream in, many too exciting to ignore. For example, in February 1961, New York City's Millrose Games created a special women's 60-yard-dash competition just so Rudolph's eager fans could see her run. The audience was not disappointed: She ran the race in 6.9 seconds, tying her own world record.

Rudolph's fame enabled her to open doors that had long been closed to female athletes. Track competition was a male-dominated world where women, whatever they achieved, were still con-

Accompanied by her proud parents, Rudolph rides down Clarksville's main street during a 1960 parade in her honor. The homecoming celebration was the first racially integrated event in the town's history.

sidered second class. Rudolph's stardom crashed the barriers of gender. She was the first woman to compete in the prestigious New York Athletic Club meet, the Penn Relays, and the *Los Angeles Times* Games.

Although she was delighted that her celebrity helped women win more respect as athletes, she soon found that her reputation also brought heightened—and sometimes unfair—expectations. After Rudolph lost a race in Los Angeles, California, sports pages ran headlines asking WHAT'S WRONG WITH WILMA?

Rudolph later wrote in her autobiog-

Rudolph crosses the finish line to set a new women's indoor track record for the 60-yard dash (left), then stretches out her arms to show the distance by which she beat the second-place finisher at the 1961 Los Angeles meet.

raphy, "Nothing was wrong. I just got beat that night, fair and square. . . . But people couldn't accept that; they figured that if I won three gold medals at the Olympics, I should be able to win in a little old meet in Los Angeles." But despite the stresses of championship,

Rudolph continued to enjoy traveling and competing.

In July 1961, she was invited to Moscow, the capital of the Soviet Union. There she equaled her previous world record for the 100-meter dash and anchored the victorious American women's relay team. And the awards kept coming, too, including the 1961 James E. Sullivan Award, given to "the amateur athlete who, by performance, example and good influence, did the most to advance good sportsmanship throughout the year."

The year 1961 also brought Rudolph "one of the most memorable things" that ever happened to her. On April 15, 1961, she and Coach Temple attended a meet in Washington, D.C. There they ran into Robert Logan, an old friend from Tennessee State who was then working for the government. Logan arranged for Rudolph to meet President John F. Kennedy.

Rudolph was stunned by the invitation to the White House and asked her mother and Coach Temple to accompany her. But when Kennedy strode into the Oval Office to meet them, all three were dumbfounded. As Rudolph later remarked, "I mean, what do you say to the President of the United States . . . Hello?" Kennedy tried to put his nervous guests at ease by suggesting that they all sit down.

But if they were confused by the protocol of greeting America's chief of state, they were stunned by what happened next. A photographer had moved Kennedy's favorite rocker in order to get a better picture, and when the president moved to sit in his accustomed spot, he missed his chair. As Rudolph described the scene in her

Rudolph signs autographs at Tennessee State. Despite all the attention lavished on her, she returned to the university to complete her education and took a part-time job in the school post office.

autobiography, "Everybody ran over to help him up, and we were mortified—I mean, how else do you react when you see the President of the United States miss his chair and fall on his behind?" Fortunately, Kennedy was unhurt: "The Secret Service men picked him up, and he was laughing. In fact he laughed so hard that he got us all to laughing." The dignity-puncturing accident certainly broke the ice, and the president chatted affably with Rudolph for a full 35 minutes.

After that climactic meeting, Wilma returned to Tennessee State. It was

President John F. Kennedy talks with (left to right) Rudolph, her mother, and Robert Logan, a Tennessee State alumnus who had arranged for Rudolph to meet the president. Kennedy told the dazzled Rudolph, "It's really an honor to meet you and tell you what a magnificent runner you are."

time, she knew, to do some hard thinking about her future. She had already triumphed in two Olympic competitions, setting standards that might be impossible to meet. Four more years of training, more qualifying trials—could she actually hope for three more gold medals? As Coach Temple had warned her, "You lose in 1964, and that's what people will remember—the losses, not the three golds in 1960."

Rudolph realized that she had to face the future squarely, "to make the decision myself, the decision on when to step down. I didn't want somebody else making it for me by beating me."

She had a major race slated for 1962, a meet pitting U.S. athletes against runners from the Soviet Union. Rudolph trained extensively for the competition, to be held at California's Stanford University. Again, Rudolph would run the 100-meter dash and then anchor the U.S. 400-meter relay team. She expected a stiff challenge from the fine Soviet athletes, especially in the difficult relay.

On the day of the race, Rudolph easily bested the Soviets in the 100-meter dash. Then came the relay; and the drama built steadily as each member of the U.S. team sprinted, finished, and handed off the baton. Finally, it was Rudolph's turn. As she described it: "I get the baton. This Russian girl is about forty yards ahead of me. I give chase, I start picking up speed, and I start closing on her. She's looking at me out of the corner of her eye, and the look is like, 'What is this? I can't believe she's closing so fast.' Well, I caught her, passed her, and won the race. That was it. I knew it. The crowd in the stadium was on its feet, giving me a standing ovation, and I knew what time it was. Time to retire, with a sweet taste."

After the race, Rudolph was mobbed by fans. Finally, the crowd of well-wishers dispersed, and she went to a bench to untie her track shoes. A little boy who had been shoved out of the way by the older fans now got a chance to approach her. He had a pencil and a scrap of paper in his hand, and he asked shyly, "Miss Rudolph, can I please have your autograph?" She smiled at him and said, "Son . . . I'll do better than that." She took off her track shoes, signed her name on both of them, and gave them to the boy.

A glorious career had ended. Rudolph had come from behind to win one last race, and she had found a way to leave an indelible impression on a young fan. And she had left on top, the same year she won the Babe Didrikson Zaharias Award, given to the most outstanding female athlete in the world.

Although Rudolph retired from competition, she continued to serve as a goodwill ambassador. In May 1963, she represented the U.S. State Department at the Games of Friendship, the largest

Although she had retired from track competition the previous year, Rudolph symboli-cally trades her running shoes for a diploma in this photograph taken on May 27, 1963, the day she graduated from Tennessee State.

Rudolph and leaders from Clarksville's black community find the door locked as they attempt to enter a segregated restaurant. They were participating in a 1963 protest that ultimately forced several local establishments to admit blacks for the first time.

track-and-field event ever held in Africa. After viewing the competition, which took place in Dakar, Senegal, Rudolph got a chance to tour the continent. She was fascinated by Africa and its people, and even took to wearing native dress during her stay. Next she joined evangelist Billy Graham in Japan, as a member of the Baptist Christian Athletes.

Her return to the United States was marred by tragedy. On the day she got back, Coach Gray was killed in an automobile accident. She was shattered by the death of the gruff but gentle man who had taught her to

95

compete, to train hard, to refuse to give up. Rudolph wanted to cancel plans she had made for yet another trip to the Orient, but, as she wrote in her autobiography, she was finally convinced that "Coach Gray would have wanted me to go—after all, he started me off on this life."

Her spirits revived by the two-month journey, she returned home to Tennessee to find two job offers waiting for her. She was asked to take over Gray's position as the Burt High School track coach that fall and also to teach second grade at her former elementary school. She had always loved Clarksville—its familiarity was a comfort and her family was there—and the offers would allow her to indulge her two loves, athletics and working with children. She gladly accepted.

Rudolph now had the chance to build a personal life, something the rigors of athletics had long prevented. Through all her years of training, of single-minded dedication, her boyfriend, Robert Eldridge, had been waiting. Finally, in the summer of 1963, she was ready to marry him. By the time of the 1964 Olympic Games, Rudolph had given birth to her second daughter, Djuana. The following year she had her first son, Robert, Jr.

Rudolph continued to work as a coach and teacher, but over time she grew increasingly frustrated by the conservatism at Cobb Elementary. As she later explained, "My idea of teaching was to bring new ideas into the classroom; after all, that's what I went to college for, to learn new ideas and methods. But [the teaching staff] wanted to stay the same, no change, and they resisted everything I tried to do."

She soon left Cobb, but she couldn't stop working altogether, even if she *had* been an international celebrity. In athletics, very often it is the promoters, not the actual competitors, who make all the profits from events. Only the shrewdest athletes are able to beat the system and see reasonable financial benefits. Rudolph was not one of them. As she ruefully noted in her autobiography, "I was strictly an amateur, in more ways than one."

Rudolph took a job in Evansville, Indiana, as the director of a community center. From there she and her family moved to Poland Springs, Maine, where she would manage the girls' physical education section of a government-sponsored recreation program.

Then, in 1967, Vice-president Hubert Humphrey invited Rudolph to participate in "Operation Champ," a project that trained young athletes in America's 16 largest ghettos. It was a perfect job—who better than Rudolph understood how it felt to be poor, with big dreams? She eagerly signed on and traveled with other athletes to cities

Martin Luther King, Jr., salutes the massive crowd that turned out to hear him address a 1963 civil rights rally in Washington, D.C. Rudolph was one of the millions of Americans who mourned King after his 1968 assassination.

Rudolph coaches her 14-year-old daughter Yolanda on the fine points of sprinting. Like her mother before her, Yolanda received a scholarship to Tennessee State and trained under Coach Temple.

shouldn't sit in judgment of anybody ... I grew up in a small, segregated Southern town, but the oppression there was nothing compared to the oppression I saw in the big city black ghettos."

The late 1960s were a time of terrible strife in American cities. Whites who resented the recent gains of the civil rights movement were striking back against blacks; blacks who were frustrated by the barriers that still existed were lashing out at whites. In the summer of 1967 the violence came to a head when Newark, Watts, Detroit, and other cities erupted in riots.

Then on April 4, 1968, Dr. Martin Luther King, Jr., the great civil rights leader, was assassinated. Amid the heightened racial tensions that followed King's murder, Rudolph and her family fell prey to an ugly incident. As she and her children stood waiting for a bus in Nashville, a white man spat at her children.

Rudolph later recalled, "I saw red. I was ready to fight him on the spot." Luckily, a bystander called the police, who arrived immediately and arrested the white man. But this concrete reminder of prejudice, coupled with King's assassination, depressed Rudolph profoundly—and showed how much more work remained before racial harmony could truly be achieved.

Her stint with Operation Champ eventually ended, and before long, Ru-

across the nation, teaching track and—just as importantly—inspiring hope in young people whose chances had been limited by poverty and prejudice.

Rudolph was moved—and frightened—by the injustice and hopelessness she saw in America's black slums. She later wrote, "After working in such places, you came away with mixed feelings, or at least the feeling that you

Long after her retirement from track, Rudolph remained in the public eye as she devoted her time and energy to programs aimed at inspiring young athletes and rectify-
ing racial injustice.

Rudolph relaxes at home with her children and husband, Robert Eldridge (right). She wrote in her autobiography that her experiences have taught her that "a family's a powerful thing."

dolph discovered that she was pregnant with her fourth child. Xurry, her second son, was born in 1971. When Xurry was old enough, Rudolph returned to work, now tackling a variety of different jobs. She worked as a commentator for West German television and radio and, in the early 1970s, organized athletic programs for Mayor Daley's Youth Foundation in Chicago. Later she served as an administrator for several learning institutions and did public relations work for banks. With her good looks and tall, graceful stature, she even modeled occasionally.

But, over the course of the 1970s, Rudolph was beginning to feel frustrated with these positions. She told

Rudolph was one of five sports stars selected by the Women's Sports Foundation as America's Greatest Women Athletes in 1984. They are, from left to right, Rudolph; tennis players Martina Navratilova, Chris Evert Lloyd, and Billie Jean King; and runner Mary Decker.

an interviewer that, sometimes, "Six months later the job suddenly disappeared, after the boss got all the publicity value out of me he could." Even on worthwhile projects, such as the Youth Foundation, she discovered she was expected to function primarily as a figurehead. Tired of having her celebrity exploited, she started her own company, Wilma Unlimited, in the late 1970s.

The founding of Wilma Unlimited marked a turning point for Rudolph. She had taken firm hold of her own future; she would no longer serve as a trophy on any organization's mantle-

(text continues on page 107)

A GLORIOUS CAREER

Throughout her career, Wilma Rudolph has received dozens of athletic awards, including her first gold medal at the 1960 Olympic Games (above). On the opposite page (clockwise from top left), she accepts the 1960 Female Athlete of the Year Award; the Babe Didriksen Zaharias Award; and the New York City Gold Medal, which she and a fellow Olympian received from Mayor Robert Wagner.

Rudolph proudly displays the James E. Sullivan Award (above). On the opposite page, she receives the Christopher Columbus Award of Genoa, Italy (top); and the 1983 Vitalis Cup for Sports Excellence.

Rudolph's impact on the world of sports—and on the lives of young athletes—endures through the work of the Wilma Rudolph Foundation, an organization that trains and encourages tomorrow's sports stars. She once said "if I have anything to leave, the foundation is my legacy."

(text continued from page 101)

piece. Instead, she became, as one journalist put it, "a one-woman corporation." She began traveling around the country, inspiring others with the story of her setbacks and successes. Rudolph was especially popular on the college lecture circuit. In 1977 she acted as a consultant during the filming of a television movie based on her autobiography, *Wilma*, which was published that same year. She was often on the road for a few weeks each month, lending her time, enthusiasm, and talent to causes she believed in. The name of her new enterprise, Wilma Unlimited, said it all. Explaining the name in 1980, she said, "I do so many things, why limit myself?"

Then in 1981, she started the Wilma Rudolph Foundation, a nonprofit organization dedicated to training young athletes. Based in Indianapolis, Indiana, the organization, which had over 1,000 participants by the mid-1980s, provides its members with free coaching in their chosen sports. The group prepares talented athletes for AAU meets, national sports festivals, and even the Olympics. As Rudolph told a journalist, the Olympics had enriched her life, and in turn she hoped "to develop other champions."

In addition, she offered aspiring athletes the benefit of her own experience in planning a life beyond a career in sports. The foundation keeps a file on every trainee, charting not only athletic performance but also academic progress. As Rudolph told a reporter, "Kids need to know that there is no such thing as a superstar. Many think that if they make it big as an athlete their worries are over. I'm here to tell you that they're just beginning."

Certainly, "The Tennessee Tornado" never rested on her laurels after her astounding Olympic victories. She went on to create a full, satisfying life, providing inspiration and help to a new generation of athletes. With characteristic modesty, she told a reporter in 1984, "I don't try to be a role model. So I don't know if I'm a role model or not. That's for other people to decide."

In July 1994, Rudolph learned that she had a malignant brain tumor. Regal and courageous to the end, Rudolph died at her home in Brentwood, Tennessee, on November 12, 1994.

Wilma Rudolph had overcome polio and risen from poverty to become the "fastest woman in the world." She had won respect for women in the male-dominated world of sports, through her own spectacular achievements. Yet, Rudolph told a journalist that she valued her own idealism as much as any of her unique accomplishments: "I just want to be remembered as a hard-working lady with certain beliefs."

FURTHER READING

Associated Press and Grolier Enterprises. *Pursuit of Excellence: The Olympic Story*, Danbury, CT: Grolier Enterprises, 1979.

Hollander, Phyllis. *American Women in Sports*. New York: Grosset & Dunlap, 1972.

Jacobs, Linda. *Run For Glory*. St. Paul: EMC Corporation, 1975.

Kiernan, John, and Arthur Daley. *The Story of the Olympic Games*. Philadelphia: Lippincott, 1973.

Rudolph, Wilma (with Martin Ralbovsky). *Wilma*. New York: New American Library, 1977.

Ryan, Joan. *Contributions of Women: Sports*. Minneapolis: Dillon Press, 1975.

Wallechinsky, David. *The Complete Book of the Olympics*. New York: Penguin Books, 1984.

CHRONOLOGY

June 23, 1940	Wilma Rudolph born in Clarksville, Tennessee
1944	Contracts polio, which partially paralyzes her left leg
1956	Begins training with Ed Temple's Tennessee State University track team
Nov. 1956	Wins bronze medal in the women's relay race at the 1956 Melbourne Olympics
July 1958	Gives birth to her first child, Yolanda
Sept. 1958	Enters Tennessee State University on a full athletic scholarship
Sept. 1960	Wins the 100- and 200-meter dashes and anchors the victorious U.S. relay team at the Rome Olympics
Feb. 1961	Ties her own world record for the 60-yard dash at the Millrose Games, a formerly all-male competition
1961	Receives James E. Sullivan Award for good sportsmanship
1962	Wins Babe Zaharias Award as most outstanding athlete in the world
	Retires from track competition after winning two races at a U.S.–Soviet meet
May 27, 1963	Graduates from Tennessee State University with a degree in elementary education
1963	Represents the U.S. State Department at the Games of Friendship in Africa
	Marries Robert Eldridge
	Begins teaching at Cobb Elementary School and coaching track at Burt High
1967	Participates in Operation Champ, training ghetto youths in track
1973	Named assistant director of Chicago mayor Richard Daley's Youth Foundation
1977	Publishes her autobiography, *Wilma*
1981	Starts Wilma Rudolph Foundation for young athletes
July 1994	Learns that she has a malignant brain tumor
November 12, 1994	Dies at her home in Brentwood, Tennessee

INDEX

INDEX

PICTURE CREDITS

Tom Biracree is the author of 34 books. A former high school coach and sportswriter, he lives with his wife, Nancy, and son, Ryan, in Ridgefield, Connecticut.

Matina S. Horner is president of Radcliffe College and associate professor of psychology and social relations at Harvard University. She is best known for her studies of women's motivation, achievement, and personality development. Dr. Horner serves on several national boards and advisory councils, including those of the National Science Foundation, Time Inc., and the Women's Research and Education Institute. She earned her B. A. from Bryn Mawr College and Ph.D. from the University of Michigan, and holds honorary degrees from many colleges and universities, including Mount Holyoke, Smith, Tufts, and the University of Pennsylvania.